StrataVarious QUILTS

9 FABULOUS STRIP QUILTS FROM FAT QUARTERS

Barbara Persing
& Mary Hoover

C&T PUBLISHING

Text copyright © 2008 by Barbara Persing & Mary Hoover

Artwork copyright © 2008 by C&T Publishing, Inc.

Publisher: Amy Marson

Creative Director: Gailen Runge

Acquisitions Editor: Jan Grigsby

Editors: Karla Menaugh and Kesel Wilson

Technical Editors: Helen Frost and Robyn Gronning

Copyeditor: Stacy Chamness

Proofreader: Alix North

Cover Designer: Christina Jarumay

Book Designer: Rose Sheifer-Wright

Production Coordinator: Zinnia Heinzmann

Illustrator: Tim Manibusan

Photography by Luke Mulks and Diane Pedersen of C&T Publishing
unless otherwise noted

Published by C&T Publishing, Inc., P.O. Box 1456, Lafayette, CA 94549

Library of Congress Cataloging-in-Publication Data

Persing, Barbara,
  StrataVarious quilts : 9 fabulous strip quilts from fat quarters / Barbara Persing and Mary Hoover.
      p. cm.
  Summary: "Using "strata panels" of fabric as the building blocks for quilts, various size blocks are cut from the pieced strip panels. The book contains 9 projects and a gallery"-- Provided by publisher.
  ISBN 978-1-57120-501-8 (paper trade : alk. paper)
  1. Patchwork--Patterns. 2. Strip quilting--Patterns. I. Hoover, Mary, II. Title.
  TT835P3521855 2008
  746.46'041--dc22
                              2007037334

Printed in China
10 9 8 7 6 5

Dedication

We dedicate this book to **Elizabeth Bryson**. She not only taught us how to sew, but also showed us, by great example, how to be fair, kind, and generous women, for she is all these things and much, much more. Simply knowing her would be honor enough, but we get to call her Mom. We love you.

Acknowledgments

We want the world to know what a great family we have. We would like to thank our sisters, Ann and Kathleen, for their free labor and tireless work at Quilt Market. And thanks to our sister Jeanne and brother Michael for their encouragement and love.

We wish to thank our favorite teacher, Joen Wolfrom. Her four-day workshop on color set us on our current crazy path. We appreciate her continued friendship, support, and encouragement. Thanks, Joen.

Also, thanks to the C&T staff. You are an amazing group of people and we are honored to be a part of this family, as well.

Barbara

I would like to thank my husband, Paul, and my sons, Kyle and Quinn; without them I would not be the person I am today. Their love, support, and encouragement, not to mention tolerance for my fabric addiction, have allowed me to be a full-time quilter. Last, but not least, I thank my sister, Mary. To be blessed with a sister who is not only my best friend but understands all my quilting ideas is priceless.

Mary

First and foremost I would like to thank my family: my husband, Eric, and daughters, Olivia and Chloe, for allowing me the time to be creative and the freedom to travel to Barbara's house at a moments notice, whenever the need arises. I love you all very much. Thanks to my best friend, Barbara, not only a great partner in crime but most of all, a great sister. She makes me look good, in more ways than one.

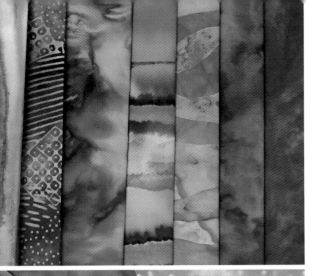

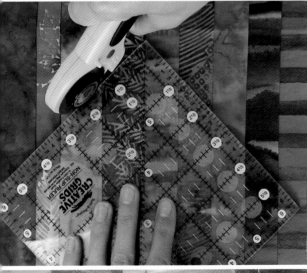

Contents

Introduction

Necessity is the mother of invention.

—Plato

How true! If you looked in our closets, you would discover that we love fabric. Wanting to incorporate as many fabrics as possible into our quilts, we began creating our own fabric designs. As we started cutting strips and piecing them back together, our first thought was "Cool! We just created fabric!" We began to fine-tune the look by playing with the strip widths. This brought the strata to life.

We don't understand the words "less is more." Our motto is "More! More!! More!!!" We love the colors, the patterns, and the values of fabric. Going to the fabric store and seeing a fabric that we just *have* to work with is the spark that starts a new fabric collection. For many years now, we've shopped for and collected fabrics. Some may say we have an addiction and need therapy, but they are the naysayers. We knew we were right all along; all the fabric collecting we've done was for a reason! Working with a large stash allows for unlimited design possibilities and is a fundamental building block of creating strata.

How can you get started creating your own unique strata? Reorganize your stash! Disregard the *styles* of fabric and sort by *color*. You will be surprised by what you see. Fabrics that you would not usually put together now look great. Fold and stack the fabric. This will give you a good indication of how the fabrics will work together in a strata panel. Continue to add fabrics to the various stacks until you have enough for your project.

Once you begin to put fabric together, it's easy to continue. One fabric leads to the next, and the next, and the next. The slight nuance of shade, tone, value, or texture adds to the overall design. This is difficult to achieve when using only a few fabrics. Variations in color bring a quilt to life and the use of many fabrics adds both dimension and depth. (See *Sweet & Sour*, page 19.)

Don't worry about the fabric leftovers! A leftover is just the beginning of a new collection. You may purchase fabrics you think will go into your current collection and then choose later not to use them. No problem! Those pieces are still loved and can be used for the next great quilt.

Why strata? Once we have a collection, we find it difficult to eliminate pieces. Every fabric in the stack has something to offer. Making strata was our solution to designing with large collections. Cutting various-sized strips created the distinct and unique blended effect we were looking for.

Making the projects in this book will teach you about strata and working with large fabric collections. This process may have you working outside of your comfort zone, and although that is not easy, it is very rewarding. What you learn will start you on your way to developing your own designs.

We have found that designing quilts does not start with a strict recipe. Be open to change and allow the quilt to develop. Many times when we start with only general ideas, collecting the fabrics will bring those ideas into focus. Going through the process of shopping for fabric and working through your stash to pull a collection together will help you become connected to the colors and ideas for your quilt. Most of all, have fun!

What are **strata**? Strata are panels of various-width fabric strips sewn together in a random manner. Each strip varies in cut width from 1″ to 2¼″. Because we start with fat quarters, strip lengths are either 18″ or 21″ long. The finished size of the strata panels will vary depending on the block size and the quilt design.

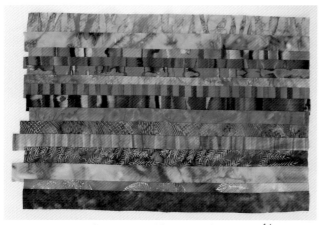

Strata panel; cut strip widths varying from 1″ to 2¼″.

Fabric Selection

Some quilters think that fabric selection is the hardest part of a project, but let us assure you that choosing fabric can be fun. Let yourself go—explore colors and fabrics that you normally wouldn't use; we strongly encourage you to work outside your usual color palette. Making projects that take us out of our comfort zones teaches us the most about ourselves as artists.

It is not difficult to put a large variety of fabrics together. Once you have found a color that inspires you and have selected your first six fabrics, you are well on your way. The next thing you know, you won't be able to stop finding fabrics to go into your growing pile.

If a pattern calls for 32 fabrics but you can find only 28, then double up on some of your fat quarters to obtain the recommended overall yardage. Your overall variety will be sufficient as long as you use at least 75% of the number of fabrics suggested.

If you're having a problem getting started, we suggest you look for pre-packaged fat quarters at your local quilt shop. Many times, two or three of these packs will go together. Leave yourself open to all possibilities. You may be amazed by what you buy and how the collection will begin to look different to you. You will also find many pieces from your stash at home that blend well with your growing selection.

Fat quarter pack

Sample fabric collection

Add large prints to the mix! Often, they will blend many of your other fabrics together and once they are cut into thin strips, they take on a new look.

Large print fabric

Large prints cut into strips and added to strata

Look for fabrics that have the same value, whether light, medium, or dark. Fabrics in the same value blend together well. When you have selected your fabrics, preview them by placing them side-by-side to see if any of them catch your eye. Those that stand out from the others will not blend well, so you should remove them from the project selections.

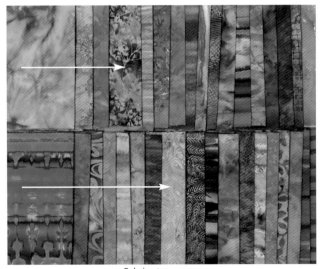

Fabrics to remove

Many of the projects in this book use contrasting colors as design elements. When choosing contrasting colors, test them by placing them on top of the strata. Remember that you want these fabrics to have a strong contrast to your background fabrics. If your fabrics don't have a strong contrast, your design will be lost.

Contrasting fabrics

Tools & Supplies

The supplies for our projects are already in most quilters' workrooms; you will need a rotary cutter, mat, and rulers to cut all the pieces and a sewing machine to piece the project. **However, you will need specific rulers for each project.**

When cutting the blocks from the completed strata, you will need to cut in all directions around the ruler. Cutting in all directions seems awkward at first, but having the correct size ruler will make learning this skill much easier. We also found that using the correct ruler will increase your accuracy considerably. Most of our projects use rulers whose outside measurements are in half inches. Once you place the ruler on the finished strata, it is best not to move it until you have cut around all four sides.

Read through the directions before beginning a project to be sure you have the necessary tools.

Cutting step 1

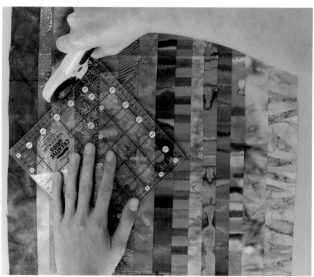

Cutting step 3

Cutting step 2

Cutting step 4

A new blade in your rotary cutter is a must! This will make it easier to make a smooth, accurate cut around your ruler.

Fabric Preparation

The big question: "To wash or not to wash?" We recommend that you pre-wash your fabrics. We use batiks in most of our quilts and we always pre-wash. We do this for several reasons:

- Some batiks have extra dye in them, so we pre-wash to remove the dye and eliminate the potential for fabric bleeding.

- Pre-washing pre-shrinks our fabrics, eliminating unwanted shrinking and distortion after the quilt is completed.

- Washing the fabric removes the sizing applied during production, leaving the fabric feeling soft. If you like to work with fabric that has a stiffer hand, we suggest using spray starch during ironing.

The most important rule about pre-washing is: *If you pre-wash one fabric, pre-wash them all.* This rule applies to the borders, backing, and binding as well. Pre-washing all the fabrics ensures they will launder the same in your finished project.

- If you choose not to pre-wash, remember to check any fabrics you select from your stash to be sure they have not been pre-washed.

- After you pre-wash your fat quarters, they may be a little smaller than 18" × 21". Don't worry about the size differences in the lengths of strips you cut for the strata. They will be fine for the projects in this book.

Cutting the Strips

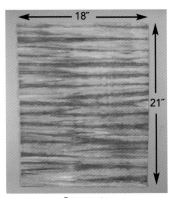

Fat quarter

Each strata panel starts the same way—cutting strips in widths varying from 1" to 2¼".

1. Cut strips in various widths from 1" to 2¼". Use the ⅛" marks on the ruler, too, for a good variety of widths. You should get 12–15 strips from each fat quarter. Each strip will be 18" or 21" long, depending on whether the strips were cut widthwise or lengthwise. Each project specifies the strip length needed. Stack up to three fat quarters and cut them at the same time. This will make the cutting go much more quickly.

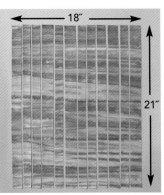

Fat quarter cut in 21" lengths. Strip widths vary from 1" to 2¼".

2. When you have finished cutting, stack each fabric. Sorting your fabrics now will keep you organized and help the piecing process go smoothly.

Sorted fabrics

Piecing

You may find that randomly selecting strips to sew together is difficult because you are used to following specific instructions. This is the beginning of letting go!

1. Piece the strips together using a consistent ¼″ seam allowance. Don't sew two of the same fabrics together and add strips of varying widths as you piece.
2. To prevent bowing, sew each seam in the opposite direction as the previous seam. Alternate between placing new strips on top of the strata and underneath the strata. This process will require you to flip the strata from top to bottom between each new strip. Continue to add strips until the strata panel is the correct width.

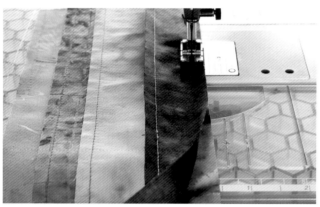

Sewing top to bottom

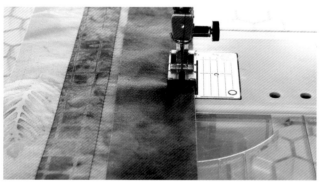

Reverse direction

Pressing

When asked what our favorite quilting tool is, we always respond with a resounding, "My iron!" Taking the time to press a seam correctly is as important as choosing your fabric, employing proper cutting techniques, and sewing a straight line. If you don't press well, it will be difficult to create accurately-sized finished blocks. Although we don't follow many quilting rules, this is an exception.

No Steam

You may use steam when you are ironing the final quilt top or after washing your fabric but *pressing seams requires no steam*. Steam creates distortion, resulting in uneven edges and warping. Invest in a high-quality iron that gets hot enough to press effectively without steam.

Let The Iron Do The Work

1. Press from the front, or the right side, of the fabric. This will ensure that the seams are as flat as they can be without creating any tucks. Pressing from the back frequently creates a crease or tuck, which presents a problem when you try to cut accurate pieces from the strata.

Pressing from the front

2. Press each seam in the same direction. We suggest that you piece a number of pairs together and then stop to press these all at the same time. You can then add the next piece to these sets and stop again later to press the new seams.
3. Now you've finished your first strata panel! The size of the strata panel will vary for each project, but the construction remains the same.

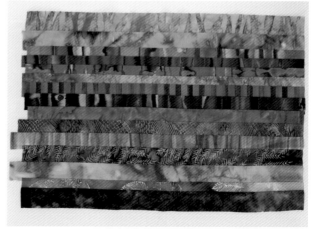

Complete strata panel

Once you've made your strata panels, it's time to cut the blocks. This is the best part about making strata quilts. Because every block will be exactly the same size, the piecing of the quilt top will go quickly and smoothly. Remember our tip—this is the time to use a new rotary blade. This will make all the difference in how easy the cutting will be.

Cutting Squares

Basic squares are used in *Fabulous II*, page 15, *Oopsy Daisy*, page 31, and *Prisma*, page 48. The example below uses a 6½″ × 6½″ square ruler, but the cutting technique is the same for any size square. The required strata panel and ruler sizes are given in each project.

 For all of our projects, you will need rulers that have an extra ½″ around the outside edge so you cut a full block without having to move the ruler. We use Creative Grids rulers, which come in a variety of sizes that include the extra ½″. (See Resources, page 63.)

1. Position the strata panel with the seams oriented vertically. Place a square ruler on the panel with the 45° mark aligned on a seam line. Cut carefully around the square. **Do not** cut to Edge A or Edge B.

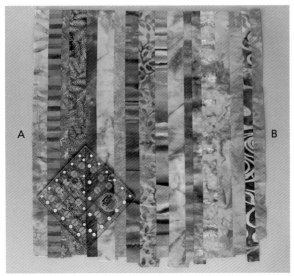

Cut around square ruler. Do not cut to edges.

2. Move the square ruler to other positions on the panel and cut additional squares, remembering to align the 45° mark on a seam line.

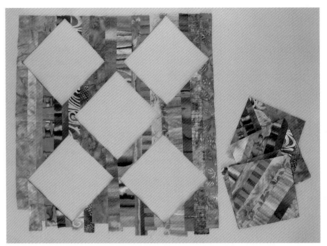

Cut more squares.

3. Use the leftover areas on the edges for another square. Sew Edge A to Edge B and cut an additional square.

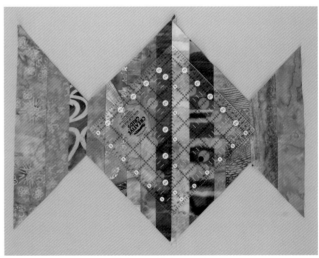

Cut one more square.

Cutting Rectangles

Cutting rectangles isn't much different than cutting squares but the slightly different shape increases your design options. Rectangles are used in *Prisma*, page 48.

Position the strata panel with the seams oriented vertically. Place a rectangular ruler on the panel with the 45° mark aligned on a seam line. Angle the ruler to the right or left. Cut carefully around the rectangle.

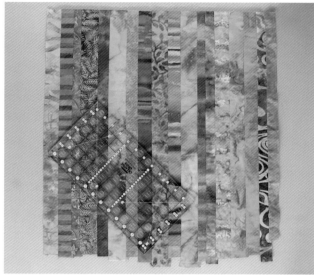

Angled left

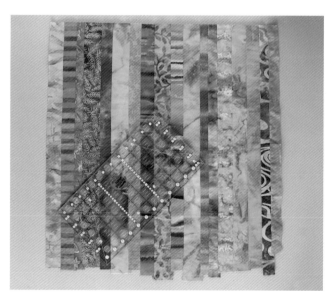

Angled right

Cutting Slanted Squares

Now you're thinking, "What could be easier than that?" Slanted squares, of course! Slanted squares are used in *Confetti*, page 24, *Gum Blossom*, page 35, and *Hop City*, page 40.

Place a square ruler on the panel at any angle, slanted to the right or the left as the pattern requires. Cut carefully around the square.

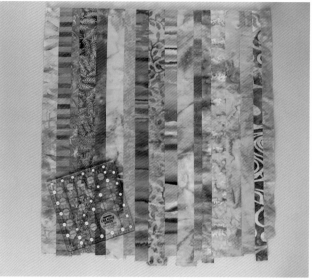

Slanted squares

Cutting Half-Square Triangles

Half-square triangles start with strata panels that are approximately as wide as the ruler you are using. Half-square triangles are used in *Sweet & Sour*, page 19, and *Energized*, page 44. The required panel size is given in each project.

1. Place a square ruler on the strata panel with some of the horizontal lines of the ruler aligned on the seam lines.

2. Cut around the square, trimming the top and bottom as necessary.

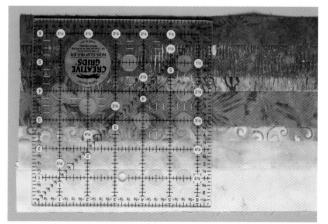

Cut the squares.

3. Cut 2 blocks per strata. Place in 2 piles, **A** and **B.** Orient the piles in the same direction.

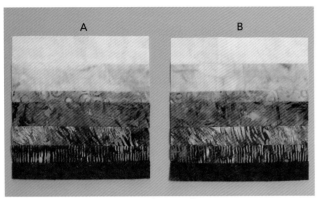

Squares in two piles

4. Cut pile A diagonally **from lower right to upper left.** Cut pile B diagonally **from lower left to upper right.**

You can stack and cut up to 3 blocks at a time, depending on your comfort level.

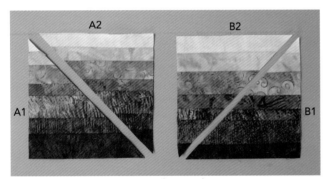

Cutting piles A and B

5. To form the new half-square triangle blocks, sew **A1** to **B1** and **A2** to **B2.** Depending on the colors and/or shading of the strata you will get 2 different squares from the same strata.

Half-square triangle blocks

Now that you know how to cut the squares, rectangles, and triangles, choose a project and get to work!

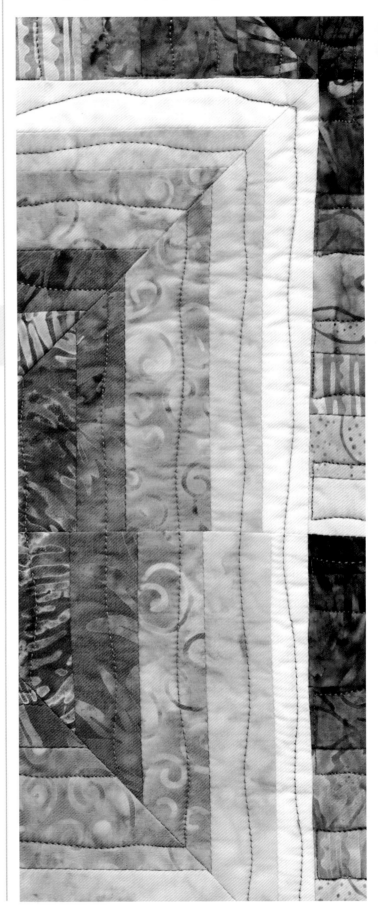

62″ × 74″
Barbara Persing and Mary Hoover
2007

We used many large prints in this quilt and encourage you to do the same. Many quilters are apprehensive about purchasing large prints. We love them because they work so well in our strata quilts. Large prints add dimension and blend well with other fabrics. See **Fabulous II: Pastel** in the Gallery, page 53, for another color variation.

Finished Quilt Size: 62″ × 74″

Finished Block Size: 12″ × 12″

Rulers:

6½″ square

7½″ square

Strata Size: 22″ × 21″

Fabric Requirements

Yellows/oranges: 15 fat quarters for strata blocks

Greens: 5 fat quarters for strata blocks

Lime green: ⅜ yard for inner border

Pinks/purples: 5 fat quarters for strata blocks

Large print: 2¼ yards for outer border

Backing: 4½ yards; pieced vertically

Binding: ¾ yard

Fabrics used in *Fabulous II*

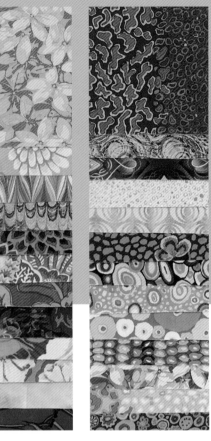

Large prints add dimension and blend well with other fabrics.

Cutting

Blocks

1. From your 5 favorite fat quarters, cut:

1 strip 9″ × 21″; sub-cut into random-width strips 1″ to 2¼″ wide and 21″ long

1 square 9″ × 9″

Set aside the rest of these fat quarters for a different project.

2. Cut the remaining fat quarters into random-width strips 1″ to 2¼″ wide and 21″ long.

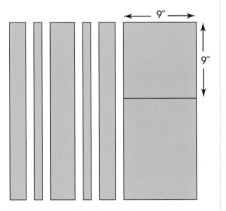

Cut 5 fat quarters.

Borders

1. From the inner border fabric, cut 7 strips 1½″ by the width of the fabric.

2. From the outer border fabric, cut:

2 strips 6½″ × 64½″ on the lengthwise grain

2 strips 6½″ × 76½″ on the lengthwise grain

Piecing the Strata

Sew various strips from all of the fat quarters together to form 12 strata panels, each at least 22″ wide. Press the seams in one direction.

Block Assembly

Square-in-a-Square Blocks

1. From each of 2 strata, cut 5 on-point squares 7½″ × 7½″ to make 10 squares total. Be sure to align the 45° mark of the ruler on a seam.

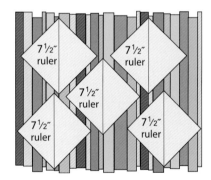

Cut on-point squares from strata panels.

 You may need to add a few strips to make these strata panels wide enough to fit 5 squares 7½″ × 7½″.

2. Using a seam ripper, carefully remove the stitches from the center seam to create 2 strata triangles from each square. Make 20 strata triangles total.

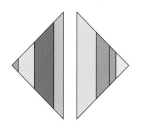

Remove stitches to create 2 triangles.

3. Sew strata triangles to 2 opposite sides of a 9″ × 9″ square, centering the long diagonal side of the triangles on the square. Press toward the triangles.

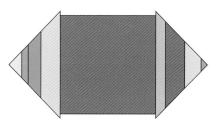

Sew triangles to opposite sides.

4. Sew triangles to both remaining sides of the square. Press toward the triangles.

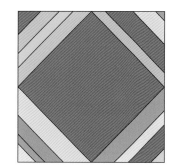

Sew triangles to remaining sides.

5. Square up the block to 12½″ × 12½″. Make 5.

 Seam intersections should be ¼″ from the raw edge.

Four-Patch Blocks

1. Cut 50 on-point squares 6½″ × 6½″ from the remaining strata. Be sure to align the 45° mark of the ruler on a seam.

2. Sew the leftover side edges of 10 panels together and cut an additional square from each. (See Cutting Squares, page 12.)

On-point square, cut 60 total.

3. Sew the 6½″ strata squares together in sets of 4 to make 15 Four-Patch blocks.

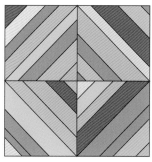

Four-Patch block, make 15.

Detail of quilting

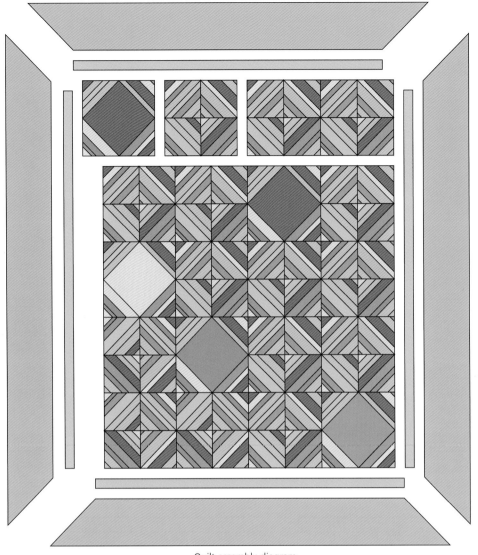

Quilt assembly diagram

Quilt Assembly

1. Arrange the blocks to form the quilt center, referring to the quilt photo, page 15, and the quilt assembly diagram, above.
2. Sew the blocks together in rows. Stitch the rows together to make the quilt center.
3. Sew 2 inner border strips together. Sub-cut into 1 strip $1\frac{1}{2}'' \times 60\frac{1}{2}''$.
4. Repeat Step 3 with 2 more inner border strips.
5. Sew 3 inner border strips together. Sub-cut into 2 strips $1\frac{1}{2}'' \times 50\frac{1}{2}''$.
6. Sew the $1\frac{1}{2}'' \times 60\frac{1}{2}''$ inner border strips to the sides of the quilt. Press toward the inner border.
7. Sew the $1\frac{1}{2}'' \times 50\frac{1}{2}''$ inner border strips to the top and bottom of the quilt. Press toward the inner border.
8. Center and sew the $6\frac{1}{2}'' \times 64\frac{1}{2}''$ outer border strips to the top and bottom of the quilt (includes 2″ for mitering). Press toward the outer border.
9. Center and sew the $6\frac{1}{2}'' \times 76\frac{1}{2}''$ outer border strips to the sides of the quilt (includes 2″ for mitering). Press toward the outer border.
10. Miter the corners.
11. See Quilting, page 58, and Finishing Up, page 62, for finishing techniques.

Sweet & Sour

60″ × 75″
Barbara Persing and Mary Hoover
2007

This is a stunning quilt using half-square triangle units. It was named by our friend, 7-year-old Aiden. He said the green looked sour and the pink looked sweet, and we agreed. See **Forest Floor** in the Gallery, page 56, for another color variation.

Finished Quilt Size: 60″ × 75″

Finished Block Size: 7½″ × 7½″

Ruler: 8½″ square

Strata Size: 8½″ × 18″

Fabric Requirements

Pinks: 20 fat quarters for strata blocks

Greens: 12 fat quarters for strata blocks

Backing: 4½ yards, pieced vertically

Binding: ¾ yard

the green looked sour and the pink looked sweet...

Fabrics used in *Sweet & Sour*

Cutting

Cut the pink and green fat quarters into random-width strips 1″ to 2¼″ wide and 18″ long.

Piecing the Strata

Sweet & Sour requires 4 different arrangements for the strata panels.

 Place an 8½″ strip of masking tape near your sewing area to use as a quick reference. You can easily see if you need to add a skinny or wide strip to the strata.

Solid Pink Strata

Sew pink strips together to form 21 strata panels, each at least 8½″ wide. Press the seams in one direction.

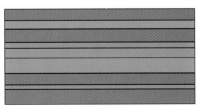

Solid pink strata, make 21.

Solid Green Strata

Sew green strips together to form 8 strata panels, each at least 8½″ wide. Press the seams in one direction.

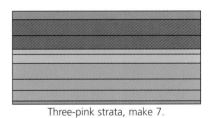

Solid green strata, make 8.

Three-Pink Strata

1. Sew 3 pink strips together. Press the seams in one direction. Make 7.

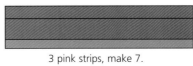

3 pink strips, make 7.

2. Add green strips to form 7 strata panels, each at least 8½″ wide. Press the seams in the same direction.

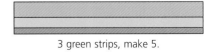

Three-pink strata, make 7.

Three-Green Strata

1. Sew 3 green strips together. Press the seams in one direction. Make 5.

3 green strips, make 5.

2. Add pink strips to form 5 strata panels, each at least 8½″ wide. Press the seams in the same direction.

Three-green strata, make 5.

Block Assembly

Solid Pink

1. Place an 8½″-square ruler on a solid pink strata. Align some of the horizontal ruler lines with the seams of the strata.

8½″ ruler

Align ruler on strata.

2. Cut around the square, trimming the top and bottom as necessary.

Cut around square.

3. Cut 2 squares per strata. Place 1 in pile A and 1 in pile B. You need a total of 42 squares; 21 squares in pile A and 21 squares in pile B.

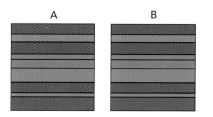
A   B

4. Cut the squares in pile A diagonally from **lower right to upper left** to form 2 triangles (these are triangles A1 and A2).

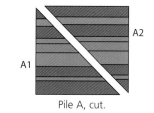
A1   A2
Pile A, cut.

5. Cut the squares in pile B diagonally from **lower left to upper right** to form 2 triangles (these are triangles B1 and B2).

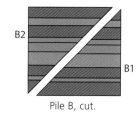
B2   B1
Pile B, cut.

6. Sew triangle A1 to triangle B1 and triangle A2 to triangle B2 to form *Sweet & Sour* blocks. Don't sew together triangles that came from the same strata square.

> **Shuffle the triangles within piles B1 and B2 to avoid sewing together triangles from the same strata square.**

Solid pink block, make 42.

7. Trim blocks to 8″ × 8″.

Solid Green

Make 15 blocks from the solid green strata, following the steps for the solid pink blocks.

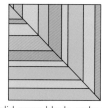
Solid green block, make 15.

Three-Pink

1. Place an 8½″-square ruler on a three-pink strata. Align some of the horizontal ruler lines with the seams of the strata.

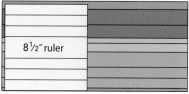
8½″ ruler
Align ruler on strata.

2. Cut around the square, trimming the top and bottom as necessary.

Cut around square.

3. Cut 2 squares per strata. Place 1 in pile A and 1 in pile B. Keep the pink strips oriented to the top. You need a total of 14 squares; 7 squares in pile A and 7 in pile B.

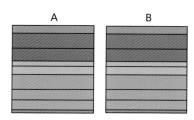
A   B

4. Cut the squares in pile A diagonally from **lower right to upper left** to form 2 triangles (these are triangles A1 and A2).

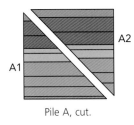

Pile A, cut.

5. Cut the squares in pile B diagonally from **lower left to upper right** to form 2 triangles (these are triangles B1 and B2).

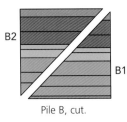

Pile B, cut.

6. Sew triangle A1 to triangle B1 and triangle A2 to triangle B2 to form *Sweet & Sour* blocks. Don't sew together triangles that come from the same strata.

Three-pink block A, make 6.

Three-pink block B, make 7.

7. Trim blocks to 8″ × 8″.

Three-Green

Make 10 blocks from the three-green strata, following the steps for the three-pink blocks. Keep the green strips oriented to the top as you place the squares in piles A and B.

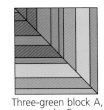
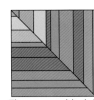

Three-green block A, make 5.

Three-green block B, make 5.

Quilt Assembly

1. Arrange the blocks to form the quilt center, referring to the quilt photo, page 19, and the quilt assembly diagram, below.

2. Sew the blocks together in rows. Stitch the rows together to form the quilt top.

3. See Quilting, page 58, and Finishing Up, page 62, for finishing techniques.

Quilt assembly diagram

Detail of quilting

56″ × 72″
Barbara Persing and Mary Hoover
2007

Blocks made from strata create the fun, free-motion background that solid squares could not. The irregular confetti pieces seem to float on a sea of vibrant blues and cool teals. See **Confetti: Green** in the Gallery, page 54, for another color variation.

Finished Quilt Size: 56″ × 72″

Finished Block Size: 4″ × 4″

Ruler: 4½″ square

Strata Size: 21″ × 21″

Fabric Requirements

Teals: 32 fat quarters for strata blocks

Lime greens: 2 fat quarters for block centers

Oranges: 2 fat quarters for block centers

Pinks: 2 fat quarters for block centers

Backing: 4½ yards, pieced vertically

Binding: ¾ yard

The irregular confetti pieces seem to float on a sea of vibrant blues and cool teals.

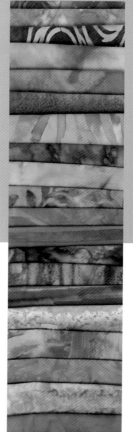

Fabrics used in *Confetti*

Cutting

1. Cut the teal fat quarters into random-width strips 1″ to 2¼″ wide and 21″ long.

2. Cut each of the lime green, orange, and pink fat quarters into the following pieces:

   8 squares 2″ × 2″

   6 squares 2½″ × 2½″

   4 squares 3″ × 3″

   Set aside the rest of these fat quarters for a different project.

Piecing the Strata

Sew the teal strips together to form 11 strata panels, each at least 21″ wide. Press the seams in one direction. Set aside the extra strips.

Block Assembly

Strata Blocks

Cut 159 slanted squares 4½″ × 4½″. Be sure to cut the blocks at many different angles. You must get a minimum of 15 squares per strata panel.

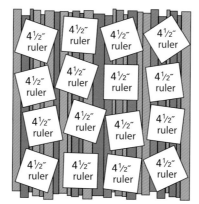

Cut slanted squares from strata panels.

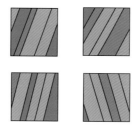

Slanted squares; cut 159.

Confetti Blocks

1. Using the leftover teal strips, randomly sew strips around 93 of the lime green, orange, and pink squares. Continue to add strips until each unit is large enough to cut a slanted 4½″ square. Make 93 units.

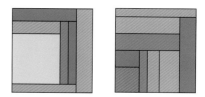

Make 93 total.

 Do not add strips equally on all sides. Add strips randomly, making some sides uneven.

2. Place a 4½˝-square ruler, angled slightly, on each unit and cut all around to make a *Confetti* block. Make 93 blocks.

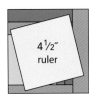

Confetti block, make 93.

Quilt Assembly

1. Arrange the blocks to form the quilt center, referring to the quilt photo, page 24, and the quilt assembly diagram, right.

2. Sew the blocks together in rows. Stitch the rows together to make the quilt top.

3. See Quilting, page 58, and Finishing Up, page 62, for finishing techniques.

Quilt assembly diagram

Detail of quilting

Neo Stella

60″ × 72″
Barbara Persing and Mary Hoover
2007

Using the strata as the appliqué adds whimsy to the otherwise traditional block. Fuchsia, pink, and orange always form a favorite color palette of ours. For a completely different look, try using earth tones as we did in **Stella Blue**, page 55.

Finished Quilt Size: 60″ × 72″
Finished Block Size: 6″ × 6″
Ruler: 6½″ square
Strata Size: 4½″ × 18″

Fabric Requirements

Light pinks: 16 fat quarters for background blocks

Pink: 1½ yards for border

Dark pinks: 9 fat quarters for strata for appliqué shapes

Oranges: 7 fat quarters for strata for appliqué shapes

Backing: 4½ yards, pieced vertically

Binding: ¾ yard

Template plastic

Fusible web (optional): 4¾ yards × 17″

Roxanne Glue-Baste-It (optional, see Resources, page 63)

Using the strata as the appliqué adds whimsy to the otherwise traditional block.

Cutting

Blocks

1. Trace the *Neo Stella* appliqué pattern, page 30, including the center line, onto template plastic. Cut on the outside line.
2. Cut 6 squares 6½″ × 6½″ from each of the light pink fat quarters. Cut 91 squares.
3. Cut the dark pink and orange fat quarters into random-width strips 1″ to 2¼″ wide and 18″ long.

Borders

Cut the border fabric along the lengthwise grain into the following segments:

    1 rectangle 6½″ × 48½″
    1 rectangle 6½″ × 30½″
    1 rectangle 6½″ × 12½″
    2 rectangles 6½″ × 18½″
    2 rectangles 6½″ × 24½″

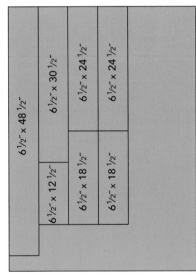

6½″ × 48½″   6½″ × 30½″   6½″ × 24½″   6½″ × 24½″   6½″ × 12½″   6½″ × 18½″   6½″ × 18½″

Cut border strips.

Piecing the Strata

1. Sew 5 or 6 dark pink strips together to form 23 strata panels, each approximately 4½″ wide, to fit the *Neo Stella* template. Press the seams in one direction.
2. Repeat with the orange strips. Make 14.

Neo Stella strata;
make 23 dark pink and 14 orange.

Block Assembly

1. Place the appliqué template on the dark pink and orange strata, aligning the center line on a seam and trace around the shape. Cut on the outside line.

Align template on seam.

2. Cut 46 dark pink and 27 orange shapes.

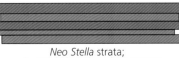

Neo Stella appliqué shape;
make 46 dark pink and 27 orange.

3. Center an appliqué shape on a 6½″ background square. Pin, glue, or use fusible web to hold in place.
4. Sew around the edge, using a buttonhole stitch or your favorite decorative stitch.

Quilt Assembly

1. Arrange the blocks to form the quilt center, referring to the quilt photo, page 27, and the quilt assembly diagram, right.
2. Sew the blocks together in rows. Stitch the rows together to make the quilt center.
3. Piece the border sections referring to the quilt assembly diagram.
4. Sew the side border sections to the quilt center. Press toward the border.
5. Sew the top and bottom border sections to the quilt center. Press toward the border.
6. See Quilting, page 58, and Finishing Up, page 62, for finishing techniques.

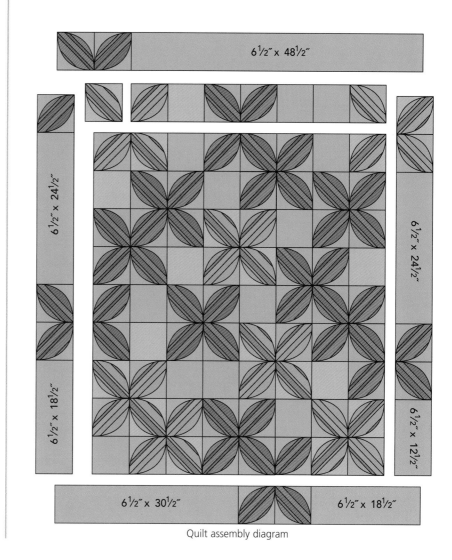

Quilt assembly diagram

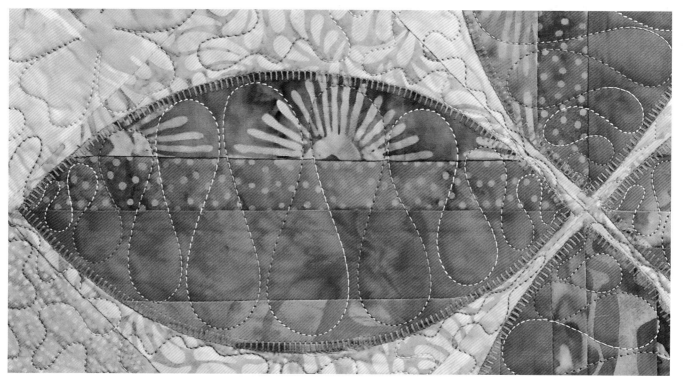

Detail of stitching

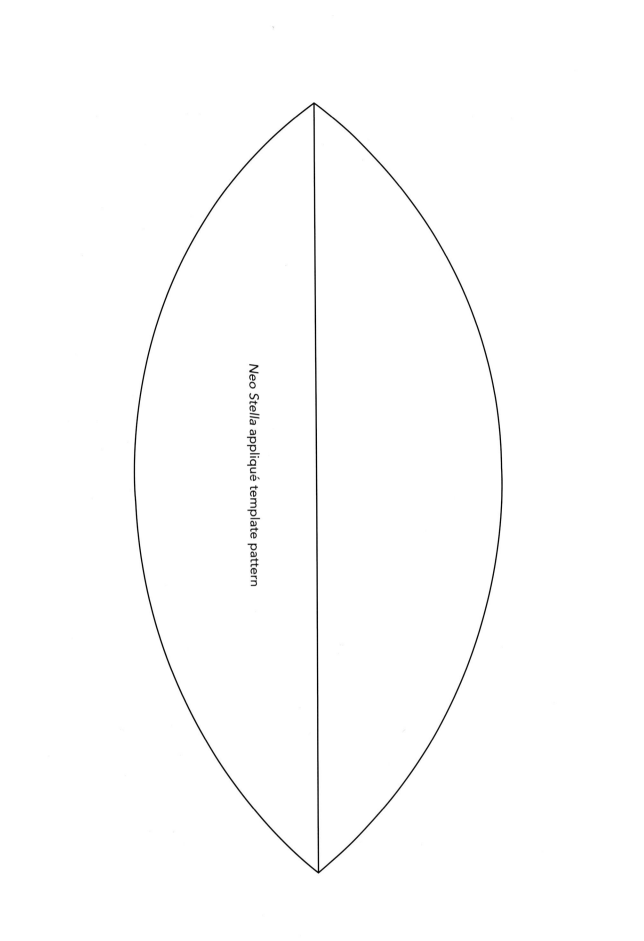

Neo *Stella* appliqué template pattern

Oopsy Daisy

48″ × 60″
Barbara Persing and Mary Hoover
2007

Appliqué is often used as the main focus of a quilt with the background remaining neutral. In **Oopsy Daisy**, the background is as interesting as the daisy itself. We found that using strata backgrounds adds a strong design element and marrying this with simple appliqué creates stunning quilts.

Finished Quilt Size: 48″ × 60″
Finished Block Size: 6″ × 6″
Ruler: 6½″ square
Strata Size: 21″ × 21″

Fabric Requirements

Blacks/grays: 25 fat quarters for strata blocks
White: ½ yard for daisy
Green: ¼ yard for stem
Yellow: scrap for daisy center
Backing: 3 yards, pieced horizontally
Binding: ½ yard
Freezer paper
Roxanne Glue-Baste-It (optional, see Resources, page 63)

Fabrics used in *Oopsy Daisy*

Cutting

Cut the black and gray fat quarters into random-width strips 1″ to 2¼″ wide and 21″ long.

Piecing the Strata

Sew the black and gray strips together to form 14 strata panels, each at least 21″ wide. Press the seams in one direction.

Block Assembly

1. Cut 70 on-point squares 6½″ × 6½″. Be sure to align the 45° mark of the ruler on a seam.

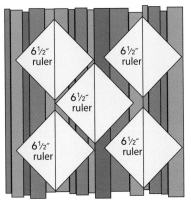

Cut on-point squares from strata panels.

We found that using strata backgrounds adds a strong design element...

2. Sew the leftover side edges of 10 panels together and cut an additional square from each. (See Cutting Squares, page 12.)

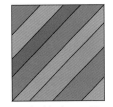

Oopsy Daisy block, cut 80 total.

Quilt Assembly

1. Arrange the blocks to form the quilt center, referring to the quilt photo, page 31, and the quilt assembly diagram, page 33.

2. Sew the blocks together in rows. Stitch the rows together to form the quilt top.
3. Layer and quilt the background. **Do not bind yet.** See Quilting, page 58, and Finishing Up, page 62, for finishing techniques.

Appliqué

1. Enlarge the pattern on page 34 400%.

 Hint A copy center with a blueprint copier can do this in one easy step.

2. Trace the daisy head, center, and stem end onto the paper side of the freezer paper. Cut the images apart. **Do not** cut the original designs.
3. Iron the freezer paper to the **right** side of the daisy, center, and stem fabrics.
4. Cut the daisy, center, and stem end shapes from the fabrics. Cut the stem by cutting a 1″ wide piece from the full width of the green fabric. It doesn't need to be straight. Use the quilt photo on page 31 as a reference.
5. Transfer all petal markings as a reference for quilting lines.
6. Glue the shapes in place using Roxanne Glue-Baste-It, using the quilt photo on page 31 as a reference. Apply glue only to the edges.

> To prevent strata seam lines from showing through the appliqué shapes, we recommend that you do not use fusible web for the appliqué in this project.

7. Using light gray quilting thread, machine stitch the lines in the center of the daisy to define each petal.
8. With matching thread, sew around the edges of the daisy petals, center, and stem. Add more details as desired.
9. Trim the quilt and bind. (See Binding, page 62.)

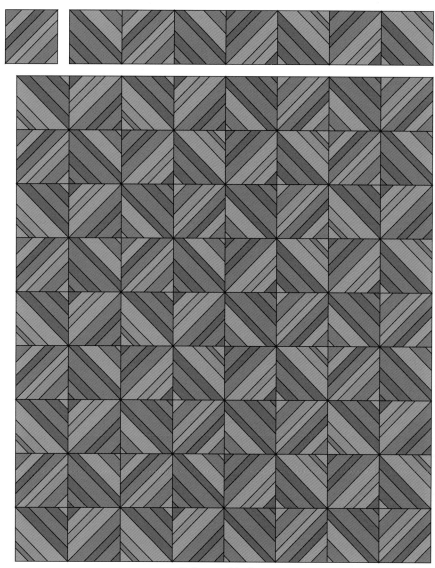

Quilt assembly diagram

Detail of quilting

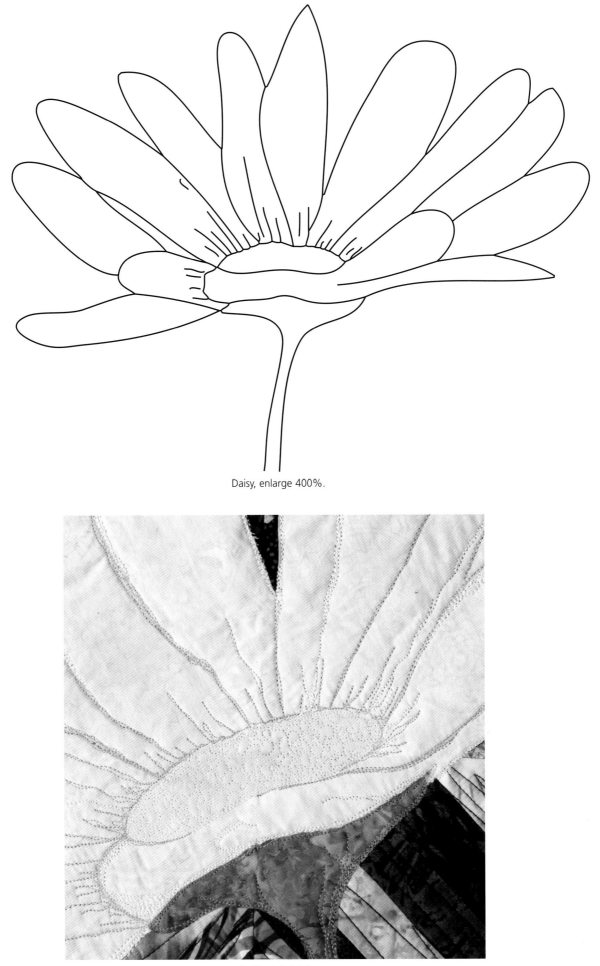

Daisy, enlarge 400%.

Quilt petal details

Gum Blossom

48″ × 42″
Barbara Persing and Mary Hoover
2007

The beauty of the gum blossom was the inspiration for this quilt. We created the soft white blossoms with thread during the machine quilting process, an easy and very effective technique. The strata background creates the same soft motion as the flowing gum blossom leaves.

Finished Quilt Size: 48″ × 42″

Finished Block Size: 6″ × 6″

Ruler: 6½″ × 6½″

Strata Size: 35″ × 21″

Fabric Requirements

Blues: 18 fat quarters for strata blocks

Light greens: 7 fat quarters for leaves

Brown: ³⁄₈ yard for stems

Tan: scraps for flower pods

Backing: 2³⁄₄ yards, pieced vertically

Binding: ½ yard

Freezer paper

Roxanne Glue-Baste-It (optional, see Resources, page 63)

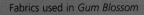

Cutting

Cut the blue fat quarters into random-width strips 1″ to 2¼″ wide and 21″ long.

Piecing the Strata

Sew the blue strips together to form 6 strata panels, each at least 35″ wide. Press the seams in one direction.

Block Assembly

Cut 56 slanted squares 6½″ × 6½″. Be sure that all of the blocks are angled in the same direction.

The beauty of the gum blossom was the inspiration for this quilt.

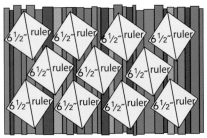

Cut slanted squares from strata panels.

Gum Blossom block, cut 56.

Detail of quilting

Quilt Assembly

1. Arrange the blocks to form the quilt center, referring to the quilt photo, page 35, and the quilt assembly diagram, right.
2. Sew the blocks together in rows. Stitch the rows together to make the quilt top.
3. Layer and quilt background. **Do not bind yet.** See Quilting, page 58, and Finishing Up, page 62, for finishing techniques.

Appliqué

1. Enlarge the appliqué pattern on page 39 500%.

 A copy center that has a blueprint copier can do this in one easy step.

2. Trace the shapes onto the paper side of the freezer paper. **Do not** cut the original designs.
3. Iron the freezer paper to the **right** side of the appliqué fabrics.
4. Cut the shapes from the fabric.
5. Transfer the leaf markings as a reference for quilting lines.
6. Glue the shapes in place using Roxanne Glue-Baste-It referring to the quilt photo on page 35. Apply glue only to the edges.

 To prevent strata seam lines from showing through the appliqué shapes, we recommend that you do not use fusible web for the appliqué in this project.

7. Quilt the background, vine, and leaves with matching thread.

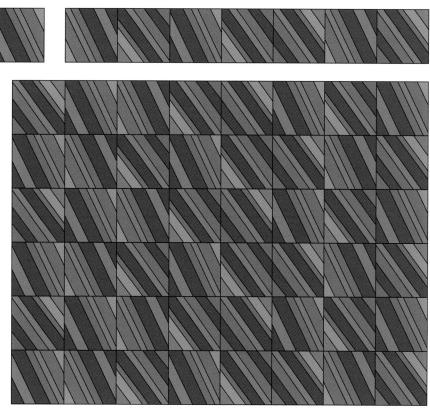

Quilt assembly diagram

8. Create the blossoms with straight-line quilting stitches referring to the photo of the flower detail, right, and the sketches of the flower head's full and side views, page 38.
   a. Start with white thread to create the shape and fullness in the blossoms. Stitch several straight lines right next to each other to create the spokes of each blossom, and stitch small circles at the end of each spoke.
   b. To highlight and soften the color of the flowers, stitch over some of the central lines of the spokes with yellow thread.
   c. To finish, stitch the center of the blossom with green thread.
9. Trim the quilt and bind. (See Binding, page 62.)

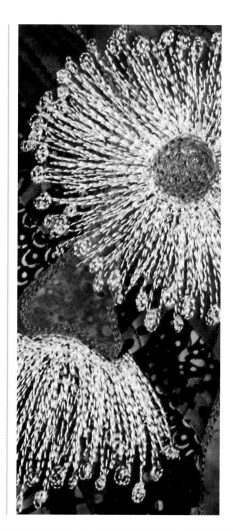

Detail of flowers

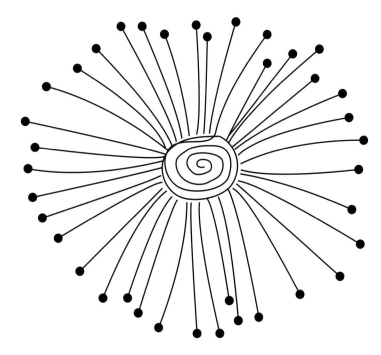

Gum Blossom head, full view, actual size

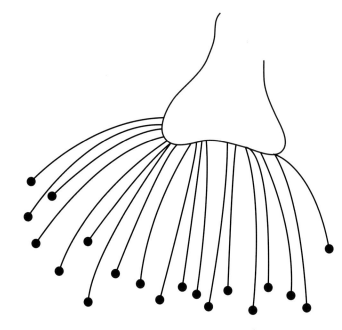

Gum Blossom head, side view, actual size

Gum Blossom appliqué template pattern. Enlarge 500%.

Hop City

48″ × 52″
Barbara Persing and Mary Hoover
2007

Stark squares set against the softness of the background colors are the simple elements in this contemporary quilt. The subtle variations in the values of the peach fabrics and the slight angles of the strata blocks produce the blended background. The high contrast between the peach, terra cotta, and plum add to **Hop City's** strong geometric design.

Finished Quilt Size: 48″ × 52″
Finished Block Sizes: 4″ × 4″, 8″ × 8″, 12″ × 12″
Rulers:
 4½″ square
 8½″ square
 12½″ square
Strata Size: 21″ × 21″

Fabric Requirements

Peach: 14 fat quarters for strata blocks
Terra cotta: 12 fat quarters for strata blocks
Plum: 10 fat quarters for strata blocks
Backing: 3¼ yards; pieced horizontally
Binding: ⅝ yard

Fabrics used in *Hop City*

The subtle variations in the values of the peach fabrics and the slight angles of the strata blocks produce the blended background.

Cutting

Cut the peach, terra cotta, and plum fat quarters into random-width strips 1″ to 2¼″ wide and 21″ long.

Piecing the Strata

1. Sew the peach strips together to form 7 strata panels, each at least 21″ wide. Press the seams in one direction. Set aside the extra strips.
2. Repeat Step 1 with the terra cotta strips. Make 6.
3. Repeat Step 1 with the plum strips. Make 4.

Block Assembly

Small **Hop City** Blocks

Cut a minimum of 15 slanted squares 4½″ × 4½″ from each strata. Be sure to cut the blocks at many different angles. Cut 102 peach blocks, 80 terra cotta blocks, and 60 plum blocks.

Cut slanted squares from strata panels.

Slanted Nine-Patch Blocks

1. Sew together a Nine-Patch block using 1 peach block at the center and 8 terra cotta blocks. Make 7.

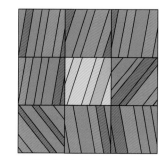

Nine-Patch block, make 7.

2. Place an 8½″-square ruler, angled slightly, on the Nine-Patch block and cut all around to make a slanted Nine-Patch block. Make 7.

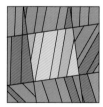

Terra cotta slanted Nine-Patch block, make 7.

3. Repeat Steps 1 and 2, using a peach square at the center and 8 plum squares to make a plum slanted Nine-Patch block. Make 6.

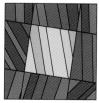

Plum slanted Nine-Patch block, make 6.

Large **Hop City** Blocks

1. Sew 2 plum squares together. Repeat, making 2 pairs.

Plum pairs; make 2.

2. Sew 4 plum squares together. Repeat, making 2 rows.

Plum rows; make 2.

3. Sew the plum pairs to opposite sides of a terra cotta slanted Nine-Patch block.

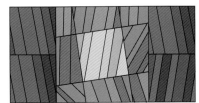

Sew pairs to opposite sides.

4. Sew the plum rows to the remaining sides of the terra cotta block.

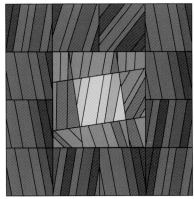

Sew strips to remaining sides.

5. Place a 12½˝-square ruler, angled slightly, on the new square and cut all around to make a large *Hop City* block.

Large plum *Hop City* block, make 1.

Detail of quilting

6. Repeat Steps 1–5, using a plum slanted Nine-Patch block in the center and terra cotta strata blocks on all sides. Make 2.

Large terra cotta *Hop City* block, make 2.

Quilt Assembly

1. Arrange the blocks to form the quilt center, referring to the quilt photo, page 40, and the quilt assembly diagram, below.

2. Sew the blocks together into sections. Stitch the sections together to make the quilt top.

3. See Quilting, page 58, and Finishing Up, page 62, for finishing techniques.

Quilt assembly diagram

Energized

38½" × 44"
Barbara Persing and Mary Hoover
2007

We love working with a graduation of color from light to dark in a single color palette—also known as a colorwash. With a colorwash of only seven fabrics and the interplay of two color families, a dynamic quilt is born. With a little manipulation of these strata blocks, an entirely new quilt emerges—a perfect example of how simplicity can be stunning.

Finished Quilt Size: $38\frac{1}{2}'' \times 44''$
Finished Block Size: $5\frac{1}{2}'' \times 5\frac{1}{2}''$
Ruler: $6\frac{1}{2}''$ square
Strata Size: $6\frac{1}{2}'' \times 21''$

Fabric Requirements

Corals: 7 fat quarters, colorwashed from light to dark, for strata blocks

Greens: 7 fat quarters, colorwashed from light to dark, for strata blocks

Backing: $2\frac{1}{2}$ yards, pieced horizontally

Binding: $\frac{1}{2}$ yard

Fabrics used in *Energized*

—a perfect example of how simplicity can be stunning.

Cutting

Cut the coral and green fat quarters into random-width strips $1''$ to $2\frac{1}{4}''$ wide and $21''$ long.

Piecing the Strata

Energized requires 10 separate strata panels from each color family.

Place a $6\frac{1}{2}''$ strip of masking tape near your sewing area to use as a quick reference. After piecing 5 strips together, measure the strata to see how wide the last 2 strips need to be.

Coral Strata

Sew coral strips together, light to dark, using various widths to form strata panels at least $6\frac{1}{2}''$ wide. Press the seams in one direction. Make 10.

Coral strata panel, make 10.

Green Strata

Sew green strips together, light to dark, using various widths to form strata panels at least $6\frac{1}{2}''$ wide. Press the seams in one direction. Make 10.

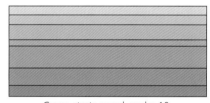

Green strata panel, make 10.

Block Assembly

Coral Blocks

1. Place a $6\frac{1}{2}$-square ruler on a coral strata panel. Align some of the horizontal lines of the ruler with the seams of the strata.

Align ruler on strata.

2. Cut around the square, trimming the top and bottom as necessary.

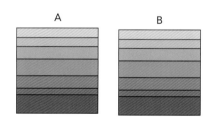

Cut around square.

3. Cut 3 squares per strata panel for a total of 30 squares.

4. Create 2 piles with 15 squares in each pile, oriented with the lightest fabrics at the top.

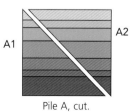

5. Cut the squares in pile A diagonally from **lower right to upper left** to form 2 triangles (these are triangle A1 and A2).

Pile A, cut.

6. Cut the squares in pile B diagonally from **lower left to upper right** to form 2 triangles (these are triangles B1 and B2).

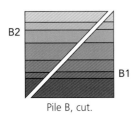

Pile B, cut.

7. Sew triangle A1 to triangle B1 and triangle A2 to triangle B2 to form coral blocks. Don't sew triangles from the same strata square together.

Shuffle the triangles in piles B1 and B2 to avoid sewing together triangles from the same strata.

Light coral block, make 13.

Dark coral block, make 15.

8. Trim blocks to 6˝ × 6˝.

Green Blocks

1. Make 13 light green and 15 dark green blocks, following the steps for the coral blocks.

Light green block, make 13.

Dark green block, make 15.

2. Trim blocks to 6˝ × 6˝.

Quilt Assembly

1. Arrange the blocks to form the quilt center, referring to the quilt photo, page 44, and the quilt assembly diagram, below.

2. Sew the blocks together in rows. Stitch the rows together to form the quilt top.

3. See Quilting, page 58, and Finishing Up, page 62, for finishing techniques.

Quilt assembly diagram

Detail of quilting

Prisma

62″ × 68″
Barbara Persing and Mary Hoover
2007

Using a rainbow as our guide, the 28 colors of this quilt flow easily together. After piecing the first strata panel and cutting some of the blocks, we were excited to see the potential in this colorwash. We easily moved the color across the quilt—it sparkled with a life of its own. This quilt is worth the effort. See **Prisma Pastel** in the Gallery, page 57, for another color variation.

Finished Quilt Size: 62″ × 68″
Finished Block Sizes: 3″ × 3″, 6″ × 6″, 12″ × 12″
Rulers:
  3½″ square
  6½″ square
  12½″ square
  6½″ × 24½″
Strata Size: various widths × 21″

Fabric Requirements

Rainbow colorwash: 48 fat quarters (28 for strata blocks, 20 for pieced outer border)
Lime green: ⅜ yard for inner border
Fuchsia: 1 yard for outer border corners
Backing: 4¼ yards, pieced vertically
Binding: ¾ yard

We easily moved the color across the quilt— it sparkled with a life of its own.

Cutting

Blocks

1. Arrange the fabrics into a rainbow of color. Number the fabrics from 1 to 28. It makes no difference where you start, but once the order is decided it must not change.

 Make a paste-up sheet to remember your fabric order.

2. Cut all of the fat quarters into random-width strips 1″ to 2¼″ wide and 21″ long.

Borders

1. From the inner border fabric, cut 7 strips 1½″ wide.
2. Number the fabrics from 1 to 20. It makes no difference where you start.

3. From each of the fat quarters, cut 5 random-width strips 1″ to 2¼″ wide and 21″ long. Set aside the rest of these fat quarters for a different project.
4. From the fuchsia border fabric, cut 4 strips 6½″ wide by the width of the fabric.

Piecing the Strata

Prisma requires 4 different arrangements for the strata panels.

Strata 1

Starting with fabric number 1 and working consecutively, sew strips together to form strata panels at least 18″ wide. Press the seams in one direction. Make 4.

 The strata panels need to be wide enough to fit a 12½″ square ruler on point. You will need 16–20 strips.

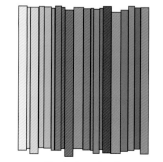

Strata 1, make 4.

Strata 2

Starting with fabric number 28 and working backward consecutively, sew strips together to form strata panels at least 18″ wide. Press the seams in one direction. Make 2.

Strata 2, make 2.

Strata 3

Starting with fabric number 1, sew strips together from 1–28 to form strata panels. Press the seams in one direction. Make 5.

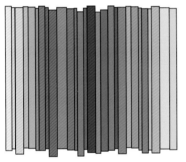

Strata 3, make 5.

Strata 4: Border Strata

Starting with border fabric number 1, sew strips together from 1–20 to form strata panels. Press the seams in one direction. Make 5.

Strata 4, make 5.

Quilt Assembly

Strata 1 and Strata 2

1. Cut 1 on-point square from each strata panel using a $12\frac{1}{2}″ \times 12\frac{1}{2}″$ square ruler. Be sure to align the 45° mark of the ruler on a seam.

2. Set aside the corner pieces for use later.

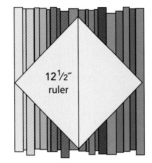

Strata 1

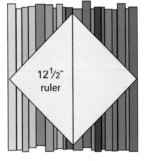

Strata 2

Strata 3

Cut the following pieces from the five **Strata 3** panels and the corners set aside from Strata 1 and 2. Always be sure to align the 45° mark of the ruler with a seam. (See Cutting Squares, page 12, and Cutting Rectangles, page 12.)

29 on-point squares $6\frac{1}{2}″ \times 6\frac{1}{2}″$
6 rectangles $6\frac{1}{2}″ \times 12\frac{1}{2}″$
28 on-point squares $3\frac{1}{2}″ \times 3\frac{1}{2}″$

Use the following illustrations as cutting suggestions.

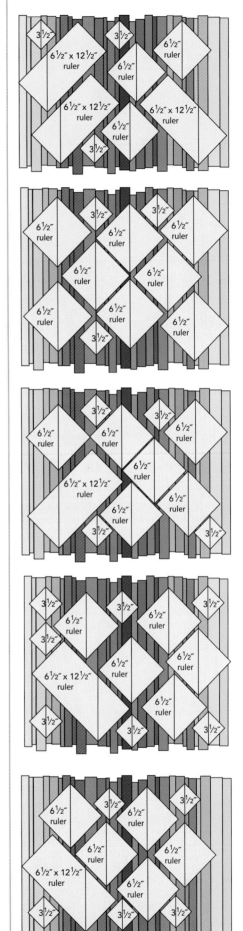

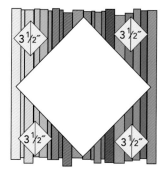

For Strata 1 and 2 leftover corners

Strata 4: Border Strata

1. With the strata oriented with fabric number 1 on the left and using a $6\frac{1}{2}'' \times 24\frac{1}{2}''$ ruler, cut 2 of the panels into $6\frac{1}{2}''$ strips. Be sure to align the 45° mark of the ruler with a seam.

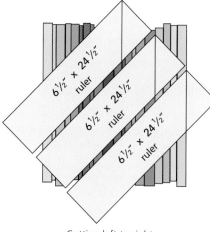

Cutting left to right

2. With the strata oriented with fabric number 1 on the left and using a $6\frac{1}{2}'' \times 24\frac{1}{2}''$ ruler, cut 2 of the panels into $6\frac{1}{2}''$ strips working from right to left. Be sure to align the 45° mark of the ruler with a seam.

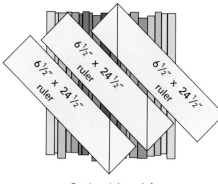

Cutting right to left

3. Cut the remaining border strata as needed.

4. Trim the ends of the strata border strips at a 45° angle to make an assortment of pieces for the borders.

Detail of quilting

Quilt Assembly

1. Arrange the blocks to form the quilt center, referring to the quilt photo, page 48, and the quilt assembly diagram, right.

2. Sew into sections. Sew the sections together to make the quilt center.

3. Sew 2 inner border strips together. Sub-cut into 1 strip $1\frac{1}{2}'' \times 54\frac{1}{2}''$.

4. Repeat Step 3 with 2 more inner border strips.

5. Sew 3 inner border strips together. Sub-cut into 2 strips $1\frac{1}{2}'' \times 50\frac{1}{2}''$.

6. Sew the $1\frac{1}{2}'' \times 54\frac{1}{2}''$ inner border strips to the sides of the quilt. Press toward the inner border.

7. Sew the $1\frac{1}{2}'' \times 50\frac{1}{2}''$ inner border strips to the top and bottom of the quilt. Press toward the inner border.

8. Sew together solid border strips and strata border strips referring to the border assembly diagram, so the longest side is at least $70\frac{1}{2}''$ (includes 2" extra for mitering). Center and sew to the sides of the quilt. Press toward the inner border.

9. Sew together solid strips and strata border strips so the longest side is at least $64\frac{1}{2}''$ long (includes 2" extra for mitering). Center and sew to the top and bottom of the quilt. Press toward the inner border.

10. Miter the corners.

11. See Quilting, page 58, and Finishing Up, page 62, for finishing techniques.

Border assembly diagram

Quilt assembly diagram

Quilt Gallery

UNLIMITED POSSIBILITIES
We created two versions of several of the quilts presented in this book.
We hope you are inspired either by the originals or those presented here.

Fabulous II: Pastel, 62˝ × 74˝, Barbara Persing and Mary Hoover, 2007

Confetti: Green, 56″ × 72″, Barbara Persing and Mary Hoover, 2007

Stella Blue, 54″ × 60″, Barbara Persing and Mary Hoover, 2007

Forest Floor, 60″ × 75″, Barbara Persing and Mary Hoover, 2007

Prisma Pastel, 62″ × 68″, Barbara Persing and Mary Hoover, 2007

Quilting

Listening to Your quilt

Now that you have finished piecing your beautiful quilt top, it's time to decide on the quilting. Barbara has been machine quilting for seven years and daily finds herself in the position of having to decide which quilting designs to use. Most of Barbara's clients want her to choose their quilting designs, so she came up with a method that makes the process easier. She takes design, balance, and thread color into consideration when choosing a quilting plan.

The goal of the quilting is not just to complete your quilt, but to have the quilt and quilting work together.

If you listen to your quilt, it will tell you what it needs. Ask yourself these questions:

1. *Will the quilting show on a busy fabric?*
2. *Does the quilting need to enhance the quilt or add dimension?*

By answering these questions, you can eliminate many quilting designs and focus your energy in the right direction.

Simple Designs

On some strata quilts, the quilting is lost in the busy fabrics and design. They need quilting that will blend with the strata and not distract from the impact of the quilt. One way to soften the look of a quilt that has sharp, square designs is by using circular quilting lines.

The easiest way to create your own quilting designs is by looking at the themes present in the quilt. Find a common motif that is repeatable and create a continuous quilting design from it.

A circular design used on *Sweet & Sour*

A square quilting design repeats *Hop City*'s square block design.

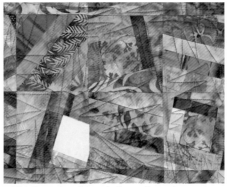

This jagged quilting design reflects the angles and movement in the *Confetti* blocks.

Circular quilting design

Continuous square design

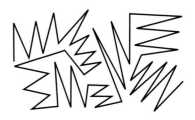

Jagged continuous design

Custom Designs

For strata quilts, custom quilting usually follows the direction of the strata. Because there are many straight lines, using soft curvy quilting lines will enhance and complement the quilt.

In *Oopsy Daisy*, page 31, the background was quilted prior to adding the appliqué. Quilting the background first made the quilting much easier, preventing stops and starts around the appliqué. Because the daisy is a large piece, the quilting is needed to define the flower.

Quilt the background first to prevent stops and starts around appliqués.

Curvy quilting lines complement strata blocks in *Prisma Pastel*.

Quilting details add definition to *Oopsy Daisy*'s large flower.

Wavy lines reflect the soft motion in *Gum Blossom*'s background.

Quilting the leaves in *Gum Blossom* creates dimension.

In *Gum Blossom*, page 35, the direction of the leaves and the angle of the strata background together create a soft gentle motion. Quilting soft wavy lines that flow in the same direction is a good example of letting the quilt speak to you.

The quilting on the leaves creates definition and dimension.

Balance

Regardless of your quilting choice, the quilting should always be balanced. This means that the density of quilting must be equal in all areas. If the quilting is dense in one area and you leave another unquilted, it will make the quilt look lumpy and uneven.

Remember to consider the whole quilting process. First, judge your skill level. A difficult quilting design may seem like a good idea, but 20 hours later when you're struggling to complete the quilt, you will not be happy. Building your quilting skills over time will prevent frustration and make you a better quilter. As with most learned techniques, time and repetition builds skill.

Next, think about a design that has minimal stops and starts. The benefits of continuous designs are not only time management, but also avoiding the knots that come from many stops and starts. Making invisible stops and starts is very important to the finished quilt.

Thread Color

The importance of thread color is frequently overlooked. You do not want to detract from your quilt by using the wrong thread color. Ask yourself if the quilt needs a contrasting thread or one that will blend. Look at the overall impact of the quilt. Is it busy or quiet? If there are interesting design elements that you don't want to detract from, use a thread that blends. The thread can still be variegated if the colors go well with the quilt. Many variegated threads were used on the quilts in this book.

An orange variegated thread picks up the colors of the *Forest Floor* blocks.

Lime-green thread variegated with orange and fuchsia picks up the mid-tones of *Prisma*.

Choosing a thread color is challenging for quilts with values that range from light to dark. When quilting *Energized*, page 44, a thread color that matched the medium color in the strata blocks was chosen. A medium-value thread is not too dark on the lightest part of the blocks and blends nicely with the remaining values.

The contrast of a dark thread on a light background not only can be distracting, it also requires perfect quilting because it will draw attention.

Once you have made all your decisions about quilting, go to it and have fun!

A medium thread color works best for quilts ranging from light to dark, like *Energized*.

Finishing Up

Backing & Batting

Remember our rule, "If you've washed one fabric, wash them all"? That includes the backing fabric.

Trim the selvages and piece together sections of fabric to make the backing a minimum of 2″ larger than the quilt top on all sides.

Cut the batting the same size as the quilt backing, allowing at least 2″ of batting on each side of the quilt.

Layering & Basting

Place the backing wrong side up on a floor or large table. Spread out the batting on top, smoothing out from the center to the edges. Center the quilt top right side up on top of the batting and backing.

Begin basting in the center and move outwards. For machine quilting, use safety pins to baste every 3″ to 4″. For hand quilting, baste with long stitches and light-colored thread.

Binding

The most common binding is a double-fold, straight grain binding, called French Fold binding, that finishes to ¼″.

1. Trim excess batting and backing from the quilt.
2. Cut strips 2¼″ by the width of the fabric. Sew together with a diagonal seam to make a continuous binding strip. Press the seams open.
3. Fold the strip in half lengthwise with raw edges even and the wrong sides of the fabric facing. Press.
4. Starting a few inches from a corner, pin the binding to a front edge of the quilt, leaving the first few inches of the binding unattached. Start sewing the binding to the quilt, using a ¼″ seam allowance.

Stitch to ¼″ from corner.

5. Stop sewing ¼″ from the corner and backstitch 1 or 2 stitches, stopping with the needle in the up position. Lift the presser foot and rotate the quilt.

6. Miter the binding strip by folding it back at a 90° angle, then fold it forward again to align it with the edge of the quilt. Put the quilt back under the presser foot and start sewing at the folded edge.

First fold for miter   Second fold alignment; repeat at all corners.

7. Stop sewing about 8″ from where you started sewing the binding. Remove the quilt from the sewing machine. Smooth the beginning and ending tails of the binding into place so you can see where they meet, putting a fold in each tail to mark the meeting point. From these folds, add 1⅛″ (half the cut width of the binding) to each tail and trim.
8. Open both tails. Place one on top of the other at right angles, right sides of the fabric facing. Mark a diagonal line from the corner of one tail to the corner of the other and stitch on this line. Trim the seam to ¼″ and press open.

Stitch ends of binding diagonally.

9. Refold the binding lengthwise and align the raw edges of the binding with the edge of the quilt top. Stitch into place.
10. To finish, fold the finished edge of the binding over the back of the quilt and hand stitch. Make a miter fold in each corner and stitch.

Resources

QUILTED HEIRLOOMS
Barbara Persing's long-arm quilting service
(610) 754-1983
www.barbarapersing.com

NINE-PATCH FABRICS
Mary Hoover's online quilt shop
www.ninepatchfabrics.com

FOURTH & SIXTH DESIGNS
(610) 754-1983
www.4and6designs.com

ADIRONDACK QUILTS
21 Cooper Street
Glens Falls, NY 12801
(800) 250-5021
www.adirondackquilts.com

CREATIVE GRIDS RULERS
Available at independent quilt shops only.
For shops in your area, see:
www.creativegridsusa.com

FLYING GEESE FABRICS
501 New Karner Road
Albany, NY 12205
(518) 456-8885

GENERATIONS QUILT SHOP
120 Shoemaker Road
Pottstown, PA 19464
(610) 718-5505
www.generationsquiltshop.com

LADYFINGERS SEWING STUDIO
6375 Oley Turnpike Road
Oley, PA 19547
(610) 689-0068
www.ladyfingerssewing.com

LITE STEAM-A-SEAM 2
The Warm Company
5529 186th Place SW
Lynnwood, WA 98037
(800) 234-9276
www.warmcompany.com

MISSION ROSE QUILTERY
456 South Main Street
North Syracuse, NY 13212
(315) 452-3247
www.missionrosequiltery.com

ROXANNE GLUE-BASTE-IT
Roxanne Products Company
742 Granite Avenue
Lathrop, CA 95330
(800) 993-4445
www.thatperfectstitch.com

STARR DESIGN FABRICS, INC.
Hand-dyed fabric
P.O. Box 440
1300 South Highway 3
Etna, CA 96027
(530) 467-5121
www.starrfabrics.com

WOODSTOCK QUILT SUPPLY
79 Tinker Street
Woodstock, NY 12498
(845) 679-0733
www.quiltstock.com

For a list of other fine books from C&T Publishing, ask for a free catalog:

C&T PUBLISHING, INC.
P.O. Box 1456
Lafayette, CA 94549
(800) 284-1114
Email: ctinfo@ctpub.com
www.ctpub.com

C&T Publishing's professional photography services are now available to the public. Visit us at www.ctmediaservices.com.

For quilting supplies:

COTTON PATCH
1025 Brown Ave.
Lafayette, CA 94549
(800) 835-4418 or
(925) 283-7883
Email: CottonPa@aol.com
www.quiltusa.com

Note: Fabrics used in the quilts shown may not be currently available as fabric manufacturers keep most fabrics in print for only a short time.

About the Authors

Barbara Persing and Mary Hoover

Photo by John T. Bollentin.

Barbara and Mary are award-winning quilt artists and their quilts have been published in many quilting magazines.

Born the fourth and sixth children in a close-knit family in south New Jersey, their mother taught these Jersey girls the art of garment sewing at the young age of ten.

Skilled in all areas of sewing, Barbara began quilting in 1983 during the long New England winters while her husband attended the University of New Hampshire. She moved to Pennsylvania in 1990 and continued quilting as a hobby. In 2000, she left the corporate world to start her long-arm quilting business, Quilted Heirlooms.

Mary began quilting in 1992 when she moved to upstate New York. As a stay-at-home mom, she needed a creative outlet and immediately knew quilting was the answer. She began teaching quilting classes in 1993 and opened a quilt shop in 1999.

Despite living 300 miles apart, Barbara and Mary began collaborating shortly after the start of their own businesses. This collaboration quickly became a partnership that has grown into the pattern and design company, Fourth & Sixth Designs. Check it out at www.4and6designs.com.

Great Titles from

C&T PUBLISHING

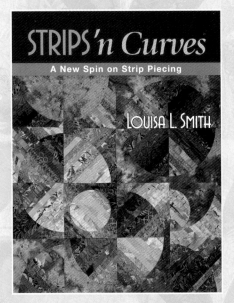

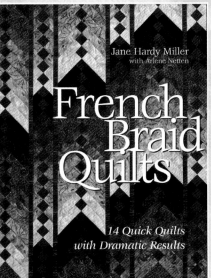
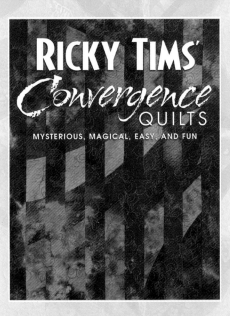